Topic 1
The US Constitution

Character

C000029131

The character of the US Constitution reflects the historical circumstances under which it was drawn up, which are summed up in this table:

1776	The 13 British colonies in North America, aggrieved by the tyrannical rule of the British monarchy, declared themselves independent.
1781	The first attempt at devising a system of government, the **Articles of Confederation**, was ratified. Influenced by suspicion of central authority, they established a loose confederation with considerable power in the hands of the 13 states and only a weak central authority.
1787	Widespread dissatisfaction with the weakness of the central government led to the calling of a constitutional convention at Philadelphia. A division quickly emerged…

1787 (cont.)	**'Federalists'**, such as Alexander Hamilton of New York, argued for the need for a stronger national government.	**'Republicans'**, led by Thomas Jefferson of Virginia, still mistrusting central government, argued for the preservation of states' rights.

Three key principles of the constitution emerged from the 'Great Compromise' between these two positions:		
The **Separation of Powers** assigns different functions to three different branches of government.	**Checks and balances** give each branch powers to check the others to prevent one becoming too powerful.	**Federalism** allows for two levels of government: the states and the federal government.

1790	Rhode Island became the last of the 13 original states to ratify the constitution.

1 **Why was it necessary to replace the Articles of Confederation with a new constitution?** `3 marks`

....

....

....

....

2 **To what extent is the division between Federalists and Republicans in 1787 still reflected in US politics today?** `2 marks`

....

....

....

3 Explain why many of the 'Founding Fathers', such as Thomas Jefferson, had such a deep and continuing mistrust of a powerful central government. **4 marks**

The separation of powers

White House

- Proposes and implements laws
- Commands armed forces
- Manages international relations and makes treaties
- Nominates Supreme Court justices and federal judges

Executive branch: President

Judicial branch: Supreme Court

- Interprets constitution
- Reviews decisions of lower courts
- Can strike down federal or state laws

Legislative branch: Congress

Supreme Court

Congress

- Passes laws
- Approves budget
- Senate ratifies treaties
- Senate approves presidential appointments
- Regulates interstate commerce
- Hears impeachment proceedings

Fotolia

The separation of powers assigns different functions to the three different branches of the federal government

Exam-style question

4 **What is meant by the separation of powers and why did the Founding Fathers introduce it?**

`15 marks` ⏱ 15

Plan your answer here then write the answer itself on a separate sheet of paper.

Checks and balances

The separation of powers is maintained by the system of checks and balances that gives each branch powers to check the others, in order to prevent one becoming too powerful.

	...Executive	...Legislative	...Judicial
Executive over...		• Can veto Acts of Congress • Responsible for implementation and interpretation of Acts of Congress • Can use signing statements to effectively reject sections of Acts • Vice president has tie-breaking vote in Senate	• Nominates Supreme Court justices and federal court judges • Has power to issue pardons
Legislative over...	• Can override veto • Can impeach president • Can reject presidential appointments • Can refuse to ratify treaties • Can conduct investigations into Executive actions • Can reject bills initiated by the president • Controls budget (purse power)		• Controls size of federal court system and number of Supreme Court justices • Can propose constitutional amendments • Can reject Supreme Court nominees • Can impeach federal judges
Judicial over...	• Can declare executive actions unconstitutional through judicial review • Power to issue warrants • Chief Justice presides over impeachment trial of president	• Can declare laws unconstitutional through judicial review • Chief Justice presides over Senate during impeachment trial of president	

5 How effective are the checks and balances between the three branches of the federal government?

45 marks   45

You should aim to write 800–1000 words. Plan your answer here then write the answer itself on a separate sheet of paper.

....

....

....

....

....

....

....

....

....

....

....

....

....

....

....

....

....

....

Federalism

Federalism is the principle that divides power between the national government and the state governments. The 13 colonies that rebelled against British rule in 1776 came together voluntarily and each had its own distinctive identity and history. The federal structure of the US Constitution was designed to enable the states to retain a high degree of autonomy, while allowing an adequately strong central government. Sovereignty is shared between the federal government in Washington and the 50 state governments.

This is quite different from countries such as Britain, where sovereignty remains in Westminster but some powers have been devolved to regional assemblies in Scotland, Wales and Northern Ireland. So, while the Parliament at Westminster could, by a simple majority vote in both Houses, claw back powers from the Scottish Parliament or the Welsh or Northern Ireland assemblies, or even abolish them, in the USA, Congress alone does not have the power to do this, as it would require a constitutional amendment.

Federalism is thus a key feature of the US political system, though the detailed nature of the relationship between the federal government and the states was left undefined in the constitution and has changed considerably since 1791. There is more about this in Topic 3.

6 Explain the reasons why the US Constitution adopted a federal structure for the government of the USA.

....

....

....

....

....

....

The Bill of Rights

The Bill of Rights is the collective name applied to the first ten Amendments to the US Constitution, which specify in some detail the rights enjoyed by US citizens and which are protected by their inclusion in the constitution. Proposed by James Madison and approved by Congress in 1789, they were ratified by three-quarters of the states on 15 December 1791. This table summarises the Bill of Rights:

1	No established religion; freedoms of religion, speech and assembly; right to petition.
2	'The right of the people to keep and bear Arms.'
3	No compulsory quartering of soldiers in peacetime.
4	Freedom from unreasonable searches and arrests.
5	No deprivation 'of life, liberty, or property, without due process of law'.
6	'The right to a speedy and public trial, by an impartial jury.'
7	Rights in civil cases.
8	No excessive fines or 'cruel and unusual punishments'.
9	The enumeration of rights 'shall not be construed to deny … others retained by the people'.
10	Powers not delegated to the federal government are reserved to the states or the people.

7 Choose one of the following Amendments and discuss modern controversies about its interpretation: 1, 2 or 8.

....

....

....

....

....

....

Exam-style question

8 How effectively does the Bill of Rights safeguard the rights of US citizens?

45 marks · 45

You should aim to write 800–1000 words. Plan your answer here then write the answer itself on a separate sheet of paper.

Amendments to the constitution

The process of making formal amendments to the US Constitution is lengthy and complex, a deliberate choice by the Founding Fathers in order to make it difficult to amend. The constitution provides for two alternative methods of amendment: through federal and state legislatures, or through specially-called Constitutional Conventions at both federal and state levels, though the latter option has only once been used.

The diagram below summarises the amendment process.

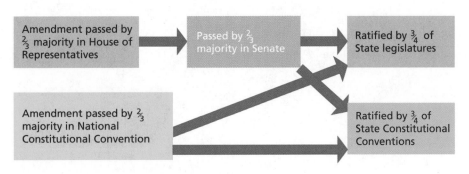

Methods of amending the US Constitution

Only 27 amendments have been ratified since the constitution became effective in 1790 and, as we have seen, ten were ratified within a year — as the Bill of Rights.

Constitutional amendment statistics

Number of constitutional amendments ratified 1790–91 (the Bill of Rights)	10
Number of constitutional amendments ratified 1792–present	17
Passed by 2/3 majority of both Houses of Congress	33
Passed by National Constitutional Convention	0
Ratified by state legislatures	26
Ratified by State Constitutional Conventions	1
Approved by Congress but not ratified by states	6

Apart from the process of formal amendment, there are ways in which the constitution has effectively changed over time. The Supreme Court has the power of judicial review, which allows adjustment of constitutional practice without going through the lengthy process of formal amendment. The very difficulty of amending the constitution greatly increases the importance of Supreme Court decisions interpreting the constitution, because reversal of the court's decision by amendment is unlikely unless there is an unusually high degree of public disagreement with it. There is more about this in Topic 4, but an example would be the court's judgment in *Brown* v *Board of Education* in 1954, which declared that segregation in schools was unconstitutional. Even unpopular court decisions (such as the court's protection of flag burning) are likely to stand unless the court itself changes its mind.

Executive and legislative practice has also changed almost out of all recognition since 1790. There is more on this in Topics 2 and 3. The following are important features of the modern American system of government but none is mentioned in the constitution: parties, primary elections, Executive Orders, signing statements, Independent Executive Agencies. This demonstrates that the US Constitution is in practice more flexible than it might appear on paper.

9 Choose two of the following Amendments:
- 25th Amendment (ratified 1967)
- 26th Amendment (ratified 1971)
- 27th Amendment (ratified 1992)
- the Equal Rights Amendment (originally proposed in 1923; not yet ratified)

Research the background to the Amendment you have chosen. Either write an answer below or do a presentation to your class on one of the two you have chosen, explaining the issue it concerns and its progress towards ratification.

10 marks

....
....
....
....
....
....
....
....
....
....
....
....
....
....
....
....

10 Why have so few constitutional amendments been made since 1791?

3 marks

....
....
....
....
....
....

Exam-style questions

11 Why did the Founding Fathers make it so difficult to amend the constitution? 15 marks (15)

Plan your answer here then continue on a separate sheet of paper.

....

....

....

....

....

....

....

12 'Outdated and ineffective.' To what extent do you agree with this assessment of the US Constitution? 45 marks (45)

You should aim to write 800–1000 words. Plan your answer here then write the answer itself on a separate sheet of paper.

....

....

....

....

....

....

....

....

....

....

....

....

....

....

....

....

....

Topic 2
The US Congress

Constitutional provision

Article 1 of the US Constitution deals with the United States Congress, which in itself is an indication that the Founding Fathers saw it as the most important of the three branches. Article 1, Sections 1 to 10 specify in some detail the procedures and powers of Congress.

1 This table summarises the ten sections of Article 1. Look up the text of the US Constitution (it is reproduced in many textbooks and is available online) and summarise the details of Article 1, Sections 2, 3 and 8, which have been left blank in the table.

3, 3 & 5 marks respectively

Section	Summary of content
1	Congress has 'all legislative powers'; consists of Senate and House of Representatives.
2	**House of Representatives:**
3	**Senate:**
4	States decide methods of election; Congress must meet at least once a year.
5	Each house to decide its own rules of procedure and to publish records of proceedings.
6	Salaries; immunity from arrest during attendance; senators and representatives barred from holding any other office.
7	Revenue bills to originate in House of Representatives; every bill to be passed by both houses and signed by the president; presidential veto powers and override procedures.
8	**The powers of Congress:**
9	Powers that Congress does not have: no suspension of habeas corpus; no ex post facto laws; limitations on powers of taxation and expenditure; no titles of nobility.
10	Powers that states do not have: no treaties with other powers; no issuing of currency; no duties on imports or exports; no keeping of troops without Congress's consent.

2 Answer the following questions about the constitution's provisions for Congress, as set out in Article 1.

a Why did the constitution originally specify that the two senators from each state should be chosen by the state legislature (Section 3)? `2 marks`

....

....

....

b Why did Sections 2 and 3 provide for different election intervals for the House of Representatives and the Senate? `2 marks`

....

....

....

c Why do you think Section 5 includes a requirement to publish records of proceedings? `2 marks`

....

....

....

d Why did Section 6 give Senators and Representatives immunity from arrest during attendance at Congress? `2 marks`

....

....

....

e Why was the power to declare war and to maintain armed forces reserved to Congress? `2 marks`

....

....

....

f What are ex post facto laws and why did Section 9 bar Congress from making them? `2 marks`

....

....

....

g Why were individual states not allowed to impose duties on imports or exports? `2 marks`

....

....

....

As we have seen, the powers of Congress are laid out in some detail in Article 1. Although the Founding Fathers intended Congress to be the pre-eminent branch, the system of checks and balances, which is referred to in Topic 1, enables the other branches to prevent Congress from becoming too dominant, and the bicameral nature of Congress means that the two Houses can act as a check on each other.

Exam-style questions

3 **Is the Senate more powerful than the House of Representatives?**   15 marks   (15)

Plan your answer here then write the answer itself on a separate sheet of paper.

4 **How effectively is Congress checked by the other branches of government?**   45 marks   (45)

You should aim to write 800–1000 words. Plan your answer here then write the answer itself on a separate sheet of paper.

Evolution

The nature and scope of legislation that Congress passes is to a certain extent shaped by the specific powers enumerated in the constitution, such as collecting taxes, regulating commerce and maintaining the armed forces. Three clauses in Article 1 Section 8, however, have proven to be sufficiently flexible to give Congress scope to expand its legislative power considerably:

- The catch-all nature of the final clause, which gives Congress 'power to make all laws which shall be necessary and proper for carrying into execution the foregoing powers' (often referred to as the 'elastic clause'), has given Congress scope to expand its legislative power. The Supreme Court sanctioned this in *McCulloch* v *Maryland* in 1819.
- Another section of the constitution whose vagueness has allowed Congress's role to grow is the interstate commerce clause. This clause allows the federal government to regulate commerce between the states and again the Supreme Court made a very wide interpretation of this in *Gibbons* v *Ogden* in 1824.

- The 'general welfare' clause, which allows Congress to collect taxes 'to provide for the ... general welfare of the United States', is a third section whose vague phrasing has allowed scope for the expansion of Congress's activities. The Supreme Court's judgement in *Helvering* v *Davis* in 1937 gave Congress wide discretion about what constituted expenditure for the general welfare.

The Founding Fathers far-sightedly gave scope for the powers of Congress to adapt to changing circumstances, making it arguably the most flexible of the three branches of government. These three crucial clauses have been used to justify the considerable expansion in the scope of the federal government, and particularly Congress, since the 1930s. A recent example is Congress's passing of President Obama's Affordable Care Act 2010, whose constitutionality was confirmed by the Supreme Court in 2012 as an extension of Congress's powers to impose taxation.

---

5 Research the details of the following Supreme Court cases, in each case explaining the implications of the judgements for Congress's power.

a *McCulloch* v *Maryland*, 1819   `3 marks`

....

....

....

....

b *Gibbons* v *Ogden*, 1824   `3 marks`

....

....

....

....

c *Helvering* v *Davis*, 1937   `3 marks`

....

....

....

....

Although the evolution process that we have considered has led to a marked expansion of the scope of Congress's legislative power over the past two centuries, there is also a case for arguing that, within the federal government, presidential power has expanded at the expense of congressional power, through the use of presidential veto powers and devices such as executive orders and signing statements. There is more about this in Topic 3.

The extent to which this has led to an 'imperial presidency' and to Congress becoming 'the broken branch' is a matter for debate. Congress has often been accused of abject and uncritical surrender of its powers to the executive branch, particularly in the field of foreign policy. There is a case for saying that, at times when the same party controls the presidency and both Houses of Congress, for example between 2003 and 2007, then congressional oversight of the executive is neglected and the legislative branch becomes too much the lapdog of the president.

On the other hand, it could also be argued that when a president faces one or both Houses of Congress controlled by the other party, Congress can become overly critical of the president in a way that is negative and destructive.

6 **Explain two examples from the past half century of Congress being (arguably) guilty of 'abject and uncritical surrender of its powers to the executive branch… in the field of foreign policy'.** `4 marks`

7 **What examples are there from the 1990s onwards of Congress being overly critical of a President from the other party 'in a way which is negative and destructive'?** `4 marks`

Power within Congress

The committee system is at the heart of Congress and congressional committees have considerable power and independence. Committees are responsible for deciding what bills and resolutions go on to be considered by the House or Senate as a whole. So the outcome of legislation is often decided within the relevant committee rather than on the floor of the House or the Senate, and committee chairs are often very powerful.

There are several types of committee: standing committees, select committees, joint committees, subcommittees, conference committees, as well as ones with special functions, such as the House Rules Committee or the Senate Judiciary Committee. There are currently 21 permanent committees in the House, 20 in the Senate and 4 joint committees.

8 **Fill in this table explaining the functions of different types of congressional committee.**

14 marks

Type of Committee	Function
Standing committees	
Select committees	
Joint committees	
Subcommittees	
Conference committees	
House Rules Committee	
Senate Judiciary Committee	

Exam-style question

9 **How important is the role of congressional committees?** `15 marks` (15)

Plan your answer here then write the answer itself on a separate sheet of paper.

....

....

....

....

....

....

....

Although committee chairs are, as we have seen, often very powerful figures in Congress, their power is rivalled by that of party leaders. Party leadership in Congress consists of the positions included in the following table.

10 **Fill in this table, putting in the name of the current holder and a brief description of the position's role. The first one has been done for you.** `20 marks`

	Office	Current holder	Description of role
Senate	President of the Senate	Joe Biden (D) (to 2017)	This position is always held by the vice president. He formally chairs Senate meetings, though may not actually attend often, and votes only when there is a tie.
	President Pro Tempore		
	Majority Leader		
	Majority Whip		
	Minority Leader		
	Minority Whip		

	Office	Current holder	Description of role
House of Representatives	Speaker		
	Majority Leader		
	Majority Whip		
	Minority Leader		
	Minority Whip		

Conventional wisdom used to be that party discipline was weak in Congress, and that representatives and senators more often voted according to their personal beliefs or the needs of their electorates, rather than on party lines. Close friendships were often formed across party boundaries, especially in the Senate, and bipartisan cooperation was frequent.

However, there has been a marked increase in partisanship in Congress since the 1970s. This can be seen in changes in party unity scores over time. Party unity scores are a measure of how frequently (as a percentage of all recorded votes) a majority of one party votes against a majority of the other party in either House of Congress. The party unity score in the House of Representatives had been as low as 27% in 1972, but had risen to the low 60s by 1992–94. In 1995, it shot up to 73% and by 2011 had reached 76%.

A key part in this growth of partisanship in Congress was played by Newt Gingrich (R), who became minority leader in 1994 and Speaker after the 'Republican Revolution' when the GOP won control of both Houses of Congress in the mid-term elections of November 1994.

11 **What changes to party organisation and partisanship in Congress resulted from the 'Republican Revolution' of 1994?**   `4 marks`

....

....

....

....

....

....

....

....

....

....

Symptoms of the increase in partisanship referred to in the previous section can also be seen in other aspects of Congress, which are also relevant to the wider question of how effectively Congress does its legislative job. These include the use of redistricting for party political advantage, the resultant decline in the number of competitive districts in congressional elections, the decline in the number of moderates of both parties in Congress, the increasing use of the filibuster and the consequent difficulty in passing legislation, resulting in near-gridlock. We shall look at each of these factors in turn and consider whether, overall, Congress is in a dysfunctional state.

⑫ What is redistricting? `2 marks`

In most states, the state legislature is responsible for the process of redistricting, but in nine states it is done by an independent commission, while the remaining seven states have only one representative, so redistricting does not arise. In states in which redistricting is done by the state legislature, this effectively means that the party in control of the legislature at the time of redistricting determines the electoral boundaries for the next ten years. If they do so in a way that benefits their own party's electoral prospects (and why wouldn't they?), this is known as gerrymandering. A notorious example of redistricting for party advantage took place in Texas in 2003.

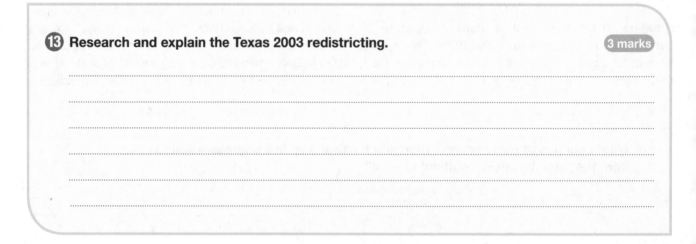

⑬ Research and explain the Texas 2003 redistricting. `3 marks`

The result of partisan gerrymandering has been that fewer and fewer congressional seats are really competitive: there is an increasing polarisation into Democrat districts and Republican districts, and a very high incumbency re-election rate. Party loyalty is often the key to candidate selection, so there has been a long-term decline in the number of moderates of both parties in Congress, as the table on the following page shows.

This growth of ideological polarisation has led to a decline in cooperation between the parties and much less bipartisan legislation. Members of both houses are increasingly engaged in work in their home districts or states (and fundraising because of the rising cost of fighting elections).

In the case of the House of Representatives, they are effectively engaged in permanent election campaigning. The increasing use of the filibuster in the Senate is another feature of recent congressional practice, which is symptomatic of partisanship and polarisation.

14 Define and explain the significance of the following terms.

a The 'Tuesday–Thursday Club' `3 marks`

....

....

....

....

....

b Bipartisanship `3 marks`

....

....

....

....

....

c Gridlock `3 marks`

....

....

....

....

....

....

Exam-style question

15 To what extent and with what consequences has the filibuster been
increasingly used in the Senate in recent decades? `15 marks` `15`

Plan your answer here then write the answer itself on a separate sheet of paper.

....

....

....

....

....

....

16 Complete the following tables, showing what happened to a number of moderates from both parties who were in the Senate in 2002. Two have been done for you.

Selected Democrat moderate senators in 2002 and their subsequent careers

Senator	State	What happened	New senator
Max Baucus	Montana		
Evan Bayh	Indiana		
Blanche Lincoln	Arkansas		
Zell Miller	Georgia	Retired 2005	Johnny Isakson (R)
Ben Nelson	Nebraska		
Bill Nelson	Florida		

Selected Republican moderate senators in 2002 and their subsequent careers

Senator	State	What happened	New senator
Susan Collins	Maine		
John McCain	Arizona	Unsuccessful presidential candidate 2008; re-elected to Senate 2010.	—
Gordon Smith	Oregon		
Olympia Snowe	Maine		
Arlen Specter	Pennsylvania		
George Voinovich	Ohio		

Exam-style questions

17 To what extent has the role of parties in Congress become more significant over the past 25 years?

15

Plan your answer here then write the answer itself on a separate sheet of paper.

....

....

....

....

....

....

....

18 How effectively does Congress scrutinise and check the executive branch of government?

45 marks · 45

You should aim to write 800–1000 words. Plan your answer here then write the answer itself on a separate sheet of paper.

....
....
....
....
....
....
....
....
....
....
....
....
....
....
....

19 'The dysfunctional branch.' Is this a fair assessment of Congress?

45 marks · 45

You should aim to write 800–1000 words. Plan your answer here then write the answer itself on a separate sheet of paper.

....
....
....
....
....
....
....
....
....
....
....
....
....
....

Topic 3
The US presidency

Constitutional provision

The US Constitution concentrates executive powers in one institution, the presidency. The powers of the presidency are spelt out in Articles 1 & 2:

Article 1
- To veto legislation

Article 2
- To be 'commander in chief of the Army and Navy of the United States'
- To 'grant reprieves and pardons'
- To 'make treaties'

- To 'appoint ambassadors, other public ministers and consuls'
- To nominate 'judges of the Supreme Court'
- To nominate 'all other officers of the United States'
- To 'from time to time give to the Congress information of the state of the union'
- To recommend to Congress legislation 'as he shall judge necessary and expedient'
- To summon special sessions of Congress 'on extraordinary occasions'
- To 'take care that the laws be faithfully executed'

---

1 Categorise these powers according to whether they are most relevant to control of the executive branch, to relations with Congress, to relations with the judicial branch, or to relations with foreign countries. **4 marks**

Control of the executive branch	Relations with Congress
Relations with the judicial branch	**Relations with foreign countries**

Veto powers

The US Constitution (Article 1, Section 7) provides that, for a bill to become law, it must be approved by both houses of Congress and presented to the president for his approval and signature. The president may sign a bill into law within 10 days (excluding Sundays), let it become law without his signature, or veto it. The constitution states that, if the president does not approve of a bill, 'he shall return it, with his Objections to that House in which it shall have originated'. This type of action is called a *regular veto*. Passage by a two-thirds majority in both houses is required to override a veto.

If, on the other hand, Congress has adjourned within the 10-day period after presentation of the bill to the president (theoretically preventing the return of the bill to Congress), the president may simply withhold his signature, and the bill does not become law, a practice known as a *pocket veto*. If a bill is pocket vetoed, Congress, being out of session, cannot override it.

2 **Compare the regular veto and the pocket veto, explaining both the advantages and the limitations of each to a president.** `4 marks`

....

....

....

....

....

....

....

....

3 **Two examples of the use of veto powers are shown in the table below. Use the internet to find two further recent examples and complete the table.** `4 marks`

President	Date	Bill vetoed	Outcome in House	Outcome in Senate
G. W. Bush	18/06/2008	HR6124, 2007 US Farm Bill	Overridden 317–109	Overridden 80–14
Obama	30/12/2009	Resolution 64, Appropriations for 2010	Override attempt failed	—

Exam-style question

4 **Why have the president's veto powers been such a battleground between the legislative and executive branches?**   45 marks   45

You should aim to write 800–1000 words. Plan your answer here then write the answer itself on a separate sheet of paper.

Informal sources of power

Apart from the formal powers enumerated in the constitution, there are a number of other factors that can enhance a president's de facto powers.

Public image and communication skills: a likeable personality, with a populist ability to connect with the public, may enhance a president's power and help him to overcome difficulties. For example, Reagan's popular homely image helped him get through the Iran Contra scandal in 1987.

Electoral mandate: a convincing margin of victory at the polls can give a president a stronger mandate and greater authority, or 'political capital', as George W. Bush put it after his 2004 victory.

Congressional support: if the president's party also controls both houses of Congress, he will find it easier to fulfil his legislative programme, although such support cannot be taken for granted.

National leader: unlike Britain, the USA does not have a monarch as a focus of national pride and unity, and to some extent the presidency provides this. It is particularly evident in times of crisis, such as Bush after the terrorist attacks in 2001.

World leader: the president's control of foreign policy enables him to project himself as an international statesman. However, foreign policy failures can also reflect badly on a president, such as Vietnam on Lyndon Johnson and the Iran hostage crisis on Jimmy Carter.

The 'institutionalised presidency': in the federal bureaucracy, the president has a huge staff effectively working for him. There will be more about this later.

5 Assess the effects, either negative or positive, of the first five factors mentioned above on the power of Barack Obama during his presidency.

`10 marks`

Continue on a separate sheet of paper if necessary.

Evolution

When the Founding Fathers were drawing up the constitution in the 1780s, they had only recently thrown off the tyranny of the British monarchy. The last thing they wanted was to create another over-powerful head of state. So a decentralised federal structure left considerable power in the hands of the states, with the powers of the presidency being checkable by Congress.

A variety of factors, however, has changed the relationship between the states and the federal government, and between the presidency and the other branches of government. The expanding size of the USA, population growth, wars, industrialisation and major national crises requiring national solutions by national government — all these factors led to a stronger central government and a more powerful presidency during the nineteenth, and especially the twentieth, centuries.

6 Give one example of a 'national crisis' from the first half of the twentieth century and outline the effect it had on the presidency.

`3 marks`

7 Explain what executive orders are and how they have been used to expand presidential power.

....

....

....

....

....

....

....

The period from the 1930s to the present has seen a struggle for supremacy between the presidency and Congress. The tide of power has ebbed and flowed between the two branches, as the timeline below shows.

President

Congress

1939: Creation of the Executive Office of the President greatly expands the number of people working for the executive branch.

1951: 22nd Amendment is ratified, limiting a president to two terms in office.

1950s and 60s: The importance of foreign policy issues during the height of the Cold War tends to tilt the balance back to the executive branch.

1964–69: The 'Great Society' increases the size and reach of the federal government.

1973: Historian Arthur Schlesinger's book *The Imperial Presidency* is published, arguing that presidential power has grown excessively.

1973: In the aftermath of the Vietnam War, Congress passes the War Powers Act, intended to prevent the president committing the USA to an armed conflict without congressional consent.

1974: President Nixon resigns following Watergate.

1980: President Ford coins the term 'imperiled presidency' to describe a weakened executive branch.

1981–89: President Reagan's ambitious agenda including tax cuts and a hike in defence spending restore presidential prestige.

1995–96: President Clinton wins a stand-off with Congress over the budget.

1998–99: The Lewinsky scandal leads Congress to impeach President Clinton, unsuccessfully.

2001–2009: The Bush–Cheney administration uses a huge increase in the use of signing statements to take presidential power to new heights.

The struggle for supremacy between the presidency and Congress, 1939–present

Exam-style question

8 **What are 'signing statements', and how significant are they for presidential power?**

15 marks   15

Plan your answer here then write the answer itself on a separate sheet of paper.

Vice presidency

The only formal duties of the vice president are to deliver a casting vote when the Senate is tied, a rare event, and to become president if the incumbent resigns or dies, happily an even rarer event. It was traditionally seen as a powerless dead-end, 'a stepping stone to oblivion', according to Theodore Roosevelt (VP 1901) and 'not worth a pitcher of warm spit', to John Nance Garner (VP 1933–41).

But the office of vice president has become much more important since the 1970s. A series of presidential candidates who were state governors chose more widely experienced running-mates who could guide them through the Washington minefield.

Dick Cheney and Joe Biden have been powerful figures in the Bush and Obama administrations, though in very different ways, leading one to the conclusion that the nature of the office today is very much in the hands of the president.

US vice presidents since 1977

Vice president	Years in office	Party	Years in Congress	Terms served	Then?
Walter F. Mondale	1977–81	Democrat	12	1	Ticket defeated in election
George H. W. Bush	1981–89	Republican	4	2	Elected president
J. Danforth Quayle	1989–93	Republican	12	1	Ticket defeated in election
Albert A. Gore Jr	1993–2001	Democrat	16	2	Became presidential candidate
Richard B. Cheney	2001–09	Republican	10	2	Retired
Joseph R. Biden Jr	2009–	Democrat	36	2	Remains to be seen

9 Choose two of the last six vice presidents. Write a paragraph explaining how each of them performed in the role.

8 marks

....
....
....
....
....
....
....
....
....
....
....
....

Exam-style question

10 For what reasons has the vice presidency become more significant in recent decades?

15 marks   15

Plan your answer here then write the answer itself on a separate sheet of paper.

....
....
....
....
....
....
....
....
....
....

Power within the executive branch

The Cabinet consists of the heads of each of the Departments of State. The four longest established departments are State, Treasury, Defense and Justice, all of which date from 1789. There are currently 15 departments, the newest being Homeland Security, established in 2003. Cabinet members are not necessarily members of the incumbent's party and do not necessarily have any previous political experience.

11 **What qualities does a president look for when choosing cabinet members?**   4 marks

Exam-style question

12 **How important a role does the cabinet play in the executive branch?**   15 marks   15

Plan your answer here then write the answer itself on a separate sheet of paper.

The *federal bureaucracy* consists of the people working for the various branches of government, some 2.7 million civilian employees, mainly professional career civil servants. Its purposes are to turn executive, legislative and judicial decisions into practical application and to assist the president in fulfilling his duty to 'take care that the laws be faithfully executed' (US Constitution, Article 2).

The president is at the centre of a large institutionalised presidency that includes the bureaucracies serving the Departments of State, the Executive Office of the Presidency (EXOP), federal corporations, independent executive agencies and independent regulatory commissions.

The bureaucracy and the number of agencies and commissions have mushroomed enormously as federal government responsibilities have grown since the late nineteenth century, especially during the Progressive Era from 1890 to 1917, the New Deal in the 1930s and the Great Society period from 1965 to 1969. The table on the following page shows selected examples of independent executive Agencies, independent regulatory commissions and government corporations.

13 Explain the functions and structure of the Executive Office of the President (EXOP).

3 marks

....

....

....

....

....

....

....

....

....

....

	Independent executive agencies	Independent regulatory commissions	Government corporations
Purpose	To serve the executive, with varying degrees of independence.	To monitor and regulate major parts of the economy.	Government-owned business corporations.
Examples	FBI NASA OPM	FEC FDA FAA	USPS TVA FNMA

14 Choose one example from each of the above three categories of institution and explain its function.

6 marks

	Independent executive agency	Independent regulatory commission	Government corporation
Example			
Function			

Federalism

As noted in Topic 1, federalism is the principle that divides power between the national government and the state governments, and is a key feature of the US political system. Yet, strangely, the constitution does not define this relationship and does not even mention the words 'federal' or 'federalism'. This has meant that reinventing federalism and the relationship between the federal government and the states has been a feature of US political life since 1791.

Date	Events
1791	The Founding Fathers envisaged a small federal government with limited powers (such as defence, foreign policy and interstate commerce) while the state governments directly governed citizens, an arrangement known as **dual federalism**. The Tenth Amendment protected states' rights: 'The powers not delegated to the US by the Constitution, nor prohibited by it to the States, are reserved to the States respectively, or to the people.'
1913	The Sixteenth Amendment allowed a federal income tax, a key change of the Progressive Era.
1930s	FDR's New Deal gave the federal government much more power, at the expense of states' rights, a rebalancing of responsibilities sometimes labelled **cooperative federalism**.
1954–69	The Warren Court issued a series of judgements with which states had to conform, beginning with the *Brown* case, 1954–55. LBJ's Great Society reforms expanded the scope of the federal government further, leading critics to talk of **coercive federalism**.
1969–89	Nixon coined the phrase **New Federalism**, promising to return powers to the states, and Reagan took this further, pledging to 'roll back the frontiers of the state'.
1989–present	Despite Clinton's declaration in 1996 that 'the era of big government is over', the need for nationally applied standards, national crises requiring national solutions, Supreme Court judgements and deliberate efforts to increase presidential power have tended to lead to power moving from states to federal government under Presidents Bush and Obama.

15 **Explain what is meant by 'New Federalism' and assess to what extent President Reagan succeeded in 'rolling back the frontiers of the state'.** 5 marks

33

16 For what reasons has power moved from the states to the federal government under Bush and Obama?

(45 marks) (45)

You should aim to write 800–1000 words. Plan your answer here then continue on a separate sheet of paper.

....
....
....
....
....
....
....

Foreign policy

The constitution divides responsibility for foreign policy between the executive and legislative branches, as the table below shows. Yet the president's position as commander-in-chief has allowed him largely to ignore congressional safeguards: 'executive agreements' take the place of treaties and the fact that the power to declare war lies with Congress (unused since 1941) has not stopped presidents committing US troops to conflicts in Korea, Vietnam, Afghanistan and Iraq.

Constitutional control of foreign policy

President	Congress
To be 'commander in chief'	To 'raise and support' armed forces
To 'make treaties'	'Advice and consent' to treaties (Senate)
To 'appoint ambassadors'	'Advice and consent' to ambassadors (Senate)
	To 'declare war'

17 Explain what the War Powers Resolution, passed by Congress in 1973, was attempting to do.

(3 marks)

....
....
....
....
....

Exam-style question

18 How effective are the checks on the president's role as commander-in-chief?   `15 marks` `15`

Plan your answer here then write the answer itself on a separate sheet of paper.

Verdict

In this topic, we have looked at the constitutional provision for the presidency, at its evolution, at power within the executive branch, at its dealings with the other branches and with the states:

- On the one hand, checks and balances still restrain the president, and the division of powers means that he must persuade the legislative branch to agree

to his policies; since the 1970s Congress, through measures such as the War Powers Resolution, has tried to increase its control over the executive branch.

- On the other hand, presidents have sought means of overcoming such restraints, such as the use of executive orders, of signing statements, and of their power as commander-in-chief.

Exam-style question

19 Which better describes the twenty-first century executive branch: 'imperial presidency' or 'imperilled presidency'?   `45 marks` `45`

You should aim to write 800–1000 words. Plan your answer here then write the answer itself on a separate sheet of paper.

Topic 4
The US Supreme Court

Judicial review

At the head of the judicial branch of the US government is the Supreme Court. As the US Constitution declares: 'The judicial Power of the United States shall be vested in one Supreme Court and in such inferior Courts as the Congress may from time to time ordain and establish.'

The main purpose of the Supreme Court is to determine whether particular laws passed by the Congress or by state legislatures, or decisions made by the executive branch, are in accordance with the constitution or not. It acts as a referee, upholding the constitution and ensuring that all the other branches do conform with it. It has the power of judicial review, enabling it to strike down acts of Congress or state laws, declaring them null and void.

It is the power of judicial review that gives the Supreme Court its political importance, since the Court often appears to be acting in a quasi-legislative manner — it can declare illegal what was previously thought to be legal, a similar effect to an Act of Congress. Although it is essentially an impartial and independent body, the Court's decisions often have political implications and may determine the outcome of highly controversial issues.

The Supreme Court has made decisions of great political importance in a range of areas, such as affirmative action (e.g. *Fisher* v *University of Texas*, 2013), abortion (e.g. *Gonzales* v *Carhart*, 2007), campaign funding (e.g. *Arizona Free Enterprise Club PAC* v *Bennett* 2011) gun control (e.g. *District of Columbia* v *Heller*, 2007) and the death penalty (e.g. *Roper* v *Simmons*, 2005).

1 **What is meant by *judicial review*?** `2 marks`

2 **Explain why the Supreme Court's power of judicial review is politically important.** `5 marks`

3 Choose two of the examples of Supreme Court cases listed on the previous page. Use the internet to research them: www.oyez.org, www.law.cornell.edu and www.scotusblog.com are useful websites. Explain what the cases were about and why they are important.

6 marks

Exam-style question

4 How extensive has the influence of the Supreme Court been on public policy in recent years?

15 marks 15

Plan your answer here then write the answer itself on a separate sheet of paper.

Just as Congress is a target for lobbyists attempting to influence legislation, so the Supreme Court is also subject to lobbying in the form of amicus curiae briefs. An amicus curiae (literally a 'friend of the court') is an individual, or a group of individuals, who is not directly involved in a court case, but who has an interest in it and who believes its views may assist the court. Rule 37 of the Rules of the Supreme Court (2010) encourages the submission of such views: 'An amicus curiae brief that brings to the attention of the Court relevant matter not already brought to its attention by the parties may be of considerable help to the Court.'

Amicus briefs come from a wide variety of sources: individuals, pressure groups, companies, states, even the federal government. A case on a controversial issue will see intense lobbying, with large numbers of rival amicus briefs from groups on both sides.

Justices frequently refer to amicus briefs in their written opinions that explain the outcome of a case. For example, in the 2003 case on affirmative action, *Grutter v Bollinger*, a brief submitted by 29 high-ranking former officers of the armed forces argued that, if affirmative action were declared unconstitutional, it would be much harder to recruit African American officers into the nation's service academies. In her opinion upholding affirmative action, Justice Sandra Day O'Connor quoted extensively from this brief, providing evidence of its crucial role in deciding the outcome.

Exam-style question

5 How significant is the role of amicus curiae briefs in the US Supreme Court?

15 marks **15**

Plan your answer here then write the answer itself on a separate sheet of paper.

Composition of the Supreme Court

The Supreme Court has a chief justice and eight associate justices, who are appointed for life. The appointment process is a lengthy and complex one:

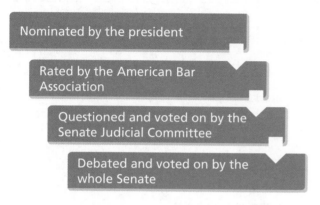

The appointment process for US Supreme Court justices

The president has to wait until a vacancy occurs through the retirement or death of one of the sitting justices. So how many justices a president is able to nominate during his four or eight years in office is a matter of chance. Confirmation is by no means a foregone conclusion: of the 24 people nominated for the Supreme Court from 1968 to 2013, a quarter were not confirmed.

6 **Describe the process by which justices are appointed to the Supreme Court.**

2 marks

....

....

....

....

7 **Why do you think the Founding Fathers involved both the president and the Senate in the appointment process for Supreme Court Justices?**

2 marks

....

....

....

....

The appointment process has become more politicised in recent years, a consequence both of the general polarisation of US politics, of the fine balance between liberal and conservative justices on the court and of the likely length of service of justices once appointed. It is not unknown for justices to continue to serve well into their 80s: John Paul Stevens was nominated in 1975 by President Ford and remained on the bench until his retirement, aged 90, in 2010. President Barack Obama's two appointments, Sonya Sotomayor (2009) and Elena Kagan (2010), may well still be on the Supreme Court a quarter of a century after Obama's departure from the White House in January 2017.

Judicial appointments thus represent an important and lasting part of a president's legacy but, once appointed, Supreme Court justices are not answerable to the president who nominated them and, while presidents generally nominate justices who share their own political and judicial outlook, they do not always get what they hope for.

Nomination process of selected recent nominees for the Supreme Court

Nominee	Year	Nominating president	ABA rating	Judicial Committee vote	Senate vote
Robert Bork	1987	Reagan (R)	Well qualified	5–9 against	Rejected 42–58
Clarence Thomas	1991	G. H. W. Bush (R)	Qualified	13–2 for	Confirmed 52–48
Ruth Bader Ginsburg	1993	Clinton (D)	Well qualified	18–0 for	Confirmed 96–3
John Roberts	2005	G. W. Bush (R)	Well qualified	13–5 for	Confirmed 78–22
Harriet Miers	2005	G. W. Bush (R)	Questionable	Withdrew	
Samuel Alito	2006	G. W. Bush (R)	Qualified	10–8 for	Confirmed 58–42
Sonya Sotomayor	2009	Obama (D)	Well qualified	18–0 for	Confirmed 68–31
Elena Kagan	2010	Obama (D)	Well qualified	18–0 for	Confirmed 63–37

8 **Choose two of the Supreme Court nominees listed in the table above. Use the internet to find out more about them. Explain the circumstances of their nomination and the process of their confirmation.**

8 marks

The table on page 40 summarises the nomination process for eight Supreme Court nominees. Note that in 1993 Ruth Bader Ginsburg was confirmed almost unanimously by the Senate, but voting on subsequent nominees has been tighter, even for those rated by the ABA as 'well qualified'. The increasing partisanship of Congress is one reason for this.

In the following passage, from the Senate's debate on John Roberts' nomination as Chief Justice of the Supreme Court in September 2005, a young Senator for Illinois gives his reasons for deciding to vote against Roberts' nomination. The Senator's views are given greater significance by his subsequent political career — his name was Senator Barack Obama:

> The decision with respect to Judge Roberts' nomination has not been an easy one for me to make... I am sorely tempted to vote for Judge Roberts based on my study of his résumé, his conduct during the hearings, and a conversation I had with him yesterday afternoon. There is absolutely no doubt in my mind Judge Roberts is qualified to sit on the highest court in the land.

Moreover, he seems to have the comportment and the temperament that makes for a good judge. He is humble, he is personally decent, and he appears to be respectful of different points of view...

The problem I had is that when I examined Judge Roberts' record and history of public service, it is my personal estimation that he has far more often used his formidable skills on behalf of the strong in opposition to the weak. In his work in the White House and the Solicitor General's Office, he seemed to have consistently sided with those who were dismissive of efforts to eradicate the remnants of racial discrimination in our political process. In these same positions, he seemed dismissive of the concerns that it is harder to make it in this world and in this economy when you are a woman rather than a man.

... I ultimately have to give more weight to his deeds and the overarching political philosophy that he appears to have shared with those in power than to the assuring words that he provided me in our meeting. The bottom line is this: I will be voting against John Roberts' nomination.

9 **Summarise in your own words the conflicting considerations that Senator Obama mentions when deciding whether to vote for or against Justice Roberts' nomination.** `3 marks`

....

....

....

....

....

....

10 **To what extent does the passage provide evidence for the increasing politicisation of the confirmation process for Supreme Court nominees?** `2 marks`

....

....

....

....

11 **For what reasons might President Obama have come to regret this speech in later years?** `2 marks`

....

....

....

Exam-style questions

12 **For what reasons have appointments to the US Supreme Court been politically controversial in recent years?** `15 marks` 🕐 15

Plan your answer here then write the answer itself on a separate sheet of paper.

13 **In what ways and how effectively is the independence of Supreme Court justices safeguarded?** `15 marks` 🕐 15

Plan your answer here then write the answer itself on a separate sheet of paper.

Judicial interpretation

The traditional view of the court's role, which is still held by more conservative justices, is that it exists simply to apply the constitution as the Founding Fathers intended. This philosophy is known as 'judicial restraint' or 'strict constructionism', because it interprets the constitution in a literal, strict or conservative manner.

Current Supreme Court justices Antonin Scalia, Clarence Thomas and Samuel Alito are often characterised as strict constructionists or conservatives. Scalia refers to his own judicial views as 'originalism', arguing that foremost in the justices' minds must always be what the writers of the constitution originally meant. For the court to do more than this is to risk making it into a dangerous rival to the legislative and executive branches.

Liberal justices, however, would argue that it is more than 220 years since the constitution was written and American society has changed enormously in that time. How can a literal reading of the constitution offer guidance on affirmative action or on President Obama's healthcare reforms, when neither concept had any meaning in eighteenth-century America? While keeping broadly to the spirit of the constitution, the Supreme Court should seek to adapt its precepts to the needs of modern America.

Examples of justices taking this view are Ruth Bader Ginsburg, Stephen Breyer and Sonia Sotomayor. This approach is known as 'judicial activism' or 'loose constructionism'.

14 **Explain in your own words what is meant by judicial restraint.** `3 marks`

15 **Explain in your own words what is meant by judicial activism.** `3 marks`

The Chief Justice most associated with judicial activism was Earl Warren (1953–69), who transformed the Supreme Court from its customary conservative stance of judicial restraint into an engine of reform, especially in the field of civil rights, in cases such as *Brown* v *Board of Education* (1954 & 1955), *Browder* v *Gayle* (1956) and *Miranda* v *Arizona* (1966). Under Warren's more conservative successors Warren Burger (1969–86) and William Rehnquist (1986–2005), the court moved back in the direction of strict constructionism, but there was not a wholesale reversal of Warren Court precedents and the Burger and Rehnquist Courts were capable of producing some liberal judgements, such as *Swann* v *Charlotte-Mecklenburg* (1971) and *Roe* v *Wade* (1973).

16 Choose two of the five classic Supreme Court cases mentioned in the last paragraph. Use the internet to find out more about them. Explain the issues involved in these cases and what the Supreme Court decided.

`8 marks`

Since 1986, the division between strict constructionists (or conservatives) and loose constructionists (or liberals) has become more pronounced. Chief Justice Rehnquist tended to ally himself with the three other conservative justices, Antonin Scalia, Anthony Kennedy (from 1988) and Clarence Thomas (from 1991). On the liberal wing were Justices John Paul Stevens, David Souter (1990), Ruth Bader Ginsburg (1993) and Stephen Breyer (1994).

A justice holding the balance between two opposing groups is often referred to as a 'swing justice' because, holding the balance of power between conservatives and liberals, he or she is often in a position to decide the outcome of cases. Sandra Day O'Connor, the first woman Supreme Court justice, nominated in 1981, increasingly filled the role of swing justice in the Rehnquist Court until her retirement in 2006.

17 Explain in your own words what is meant by a 'swing justice' and why they can be very powerful in the Supreme Court.

`3 marks`

18 The use of terms such as 'balance of power', 'liberal' and 'conservative' makes Supreme Court justices sound like politicians. To what extent is this true?

`3 marks`

The Roberts Court

The Supreme Court 2014

Justice	Born	Appointed	Nominating president	Judicial politics
John Roberts (Chief)	1955	2005	G. W. Bush (R)	Conservative
Antonin Scalia	1936	1986	Reagan (R)	Conservative
Anthony Kennedy	1936	1988	Reagan (R)	Conservative/Swing
Clarence Thomas	1948	1991	G. H. W. Bush (R)	Conservative
Ruth Bader Ginsburg	1933	1993	Clinton (D)	Liberal
Stephen Breyer	1938	1994	Clinton (D)	Liberal
Samuel Alito	1950	2006	G. W. Bush (R)	Conservative
Sonya Sotomayor	1954	2009	Obama (D)	Liberal
Elena Kagan	1960	2010	Obama (D)	Liberal

19 Look at the table showing the composition of the Court in 2014. How significant are the party allegiances of the presidents who appointed the justices? **4 marks**

After more than a decade with no changes, two vacancies occurred in quick succession in the autumn of 2005. The nomination by President George W. Bush of John Roberts, a conservative, as Chief Justice after Rehnquist's death in September 2005, left the balance more or less unaffected, but the replacement of swing justice Sandra Day O'Connor by the solidly conservative Samuel Alito in 2006 was widely regarded as a significant shift. It left Anthony Kennedy, certainly more conservative than O'Connor, as her replacement in the role of swing justice, indicating that the centre of gravity of the court had moved in a conservative direction.

President Barack Obama had his first opportunity to make a nomination to the Supreme Court in 2009

when Justice David Souter announced his retirement. Obama nominated Sonya Sotomayor, who became the first Hispanic Supreme Court justice. The retirement of nonagenarian John Paul Stevens in 2010, after 35 years on the court, allowed President Obama to nominate another Supreme Court justice. He chose Elena Kagan, Solicitor-General in his own administration.

The nominations of Sotomayor and Kagan brought the number of women on the court to three, the highest ever. Obama had begun the rejuvenation of the court's liberal wing, but neither nomination altered the ideological balance of the bench, as in each case a liberal replaced a liberal.

20 Explain in your own words the effects on the Supreme Court of appointments since 2005.

`4 marks`

....

....

....

....

....

....

....

Some liberals have demonised the Roberts Court as excessively conservative in its judgements. Ronald Dworkin accused the court in 2007 of 'the continuing subversion of the American constitution'. How far does an assessment of the Roberts Court's record support this view?

Certainly some decisions by the Roberts Court suggest a move to the right. One of the most controversial is *Citizens United* v *Federal Electoral Commission* (2010), which struck down key sections of the McCain-Feingold Act of 2002 limiting corporate funding of political broadcasts. In his State of the Union address a few days after the verdict, President Obama publicly criticised this ruling with several Supreme Court justices present, including Chief Justice Roberts. The court, he said, had 'given a green light to a new stampede of special interest money in our politics'. This case was a 5–4 majority decision, with the four conservative justices voting one way and the four-strong liberal group the other. Justice Anthony Kennedy, the swing justice, held the balance between the two opposing groups and in *Citizens United* he sided with the conservative group.

Yet by no means all the Roberts Court's decisions have been so conservative. In *ACA Cases* (2012), the court upheld as constitutional the Affordable Care Act, the Obama administration's healthcare reform, popularly known as 'Obamacare'. Chief Justice Roberts surprisingly sided with the four liberal justices, declaring that, although the Commerce Clause did not protect the law, the penalty to be imposed on citizens who failed to buy health insurance was constitutional as a tax, thus upholding the 'individual mandate', a central principle of the reform.

21 Research the cases named below: use www.oyez.org, www.law.cornell.edu and www.scotusblog.com. In each case, explain briefly the issue at stake and say whether the Roberts Court's verdict can be considered liberal or conservative.

`18 marks`

Case	Issue at stake	Verdict: liberal or conservative?
Hamdan v *Rumsfeld* (2006)		
Ledbetter v *Goodyear* (2007)		

Case	Issue at stake	Verdict: liberal or conservative?
Ricci v *DeStefano* (2009)		
McDonald v *Chicago* (2010)		
Arizona v *USA* (2012)		
Windsor v *United States* (2013)		

Exam-style questions

22 **To what extent has the Supreme Court become excessively political in recent years, to the detriment of its judicial function?**

45 marks   45

You should aim to write 800–1000 words. Plan your answer here then write the answer itself on a separate sheet of paper.

23 **Is the Supreme Court more or less powerful than Congress?** `45 marks` `45`

To answer this question, you need to make use of your knowledge of Congress and the US Constitution in general, as well as of the Supreme Court. You should aim to write 800–1000 words. Plan your answer here then write the answer itself on a separate sheet of paper.

....
....
....
....
....
....
....
....
....
....
....
....
....
....
....
....
....
....

Philip Allan, an imprint of Hodder Education, an Hachette UK company, Market Place, Deddington, Oxfordshire, OX15 0SE

Orders
Bookpoint Ltd, 130 Milton Park, Abingdon, Oxfordshire OX14 4SB
tel: 01235 827827
fax: 01235 400401
e-mail: education@bookpoint.co.uk

Lines are open 9.00 a.m.–5.00 p.m., Monday to Saturday, with a 24-hour message answering service. You can also order through **www.hoddereducation.co.uk**

© Mark Rathbone 2014
ISBN 978-1-4441-9997-0
First printed 2014
Impression number 5 4 3 2 1
Year 2019 2018 2017 2016 2015 2014

Cover photo reproduced by permission of Jonathan Stutz/fotolia

Printed in Dubai

Hachette UK's policy is to use papers that are natural, renewable and recyclable products and made from wood grown in sustainable forests. The logging and manufacturing processes are expected to conform to the environmental regulations of the country of origin.

P2290

ISBN 978-1-4441-9997-0